RUSTED FENCE

AND

BROKEN

COWBOYS

The Poetic Musings of a Misfit

RUSTED FENCE

AND

BROKEN

COWBOYS

The Poetic Musings of a Misfit

KIRBY JONAS

Cover design by Clay Jonas

Howling Wolf Publishing
Pocatello, Idaho

Howling Wolf Publishing
1611 City Creek Road
Pocatello ID 83204

For more information about Kirby's books, check out:

www.kirbyjonas.com
Facebook, at KirbyJonasauthor

Or email Kirby at: **kirby@kirbyjonas.com**

Manufactured in the United States of America—*One nation, under God*

Publication date: April 2021
Jonas, Kirby, 1965—
Rusted Fence and Broken Cowboys / by Kirby Jonas.

ISBN: 978-1-891423-40-6

Library of Congress Control Number: 2021900266

To learn more about this book or any other Kirby Jonas book, email Kirby at kirby@kirbyjonas.com

To Chris LeDoux, Marty Robbins, and Don Edwards, and all of the cowboy singers and poets who have brought me to where I am today

BROKE BONES

AND

UNBROKE HORSES

Rusted Fence and Broken Cowboys

Wind plays on the bobwire
And makes a fence post sway;
It was bull-strong, hog-tight
And horse high, in a better day.

Now the cows just pity it,
And feel too bad to cross;
In earlier days it was like a dare
To a wily cow or hoss.

Half the posts are leaning,
Their bottoms full of rot
The wire's nearly rust plumb through—
The whole fence line is shot.

The old cowboy is wearing pants
More patch than blue jean fabric;
He's limping on a thrice-broke leg
And his story's next to tragic.

He lived a cowman's dream,
Back about eighty-five;
Running a thousand Herefords,
Feeling vibrant and alive.

He had five growing children,
And a loving, lovely wife,
The best horse string anywhere,
And a most idyllic life.

And then came the Big Die-Up,
And the ranges turned to dust;
The cattle turned to skeletons,
And the windmill turned to rust.

He was one tough cowboy,
And he'd have made it through,
But sickness took his children,
Then took his woman too.

The Die-Up took his herd entire,
And even took his horses;
And men who can't live in a town
Know too well what their course is.

So he took to running mustangs,
Too plain proud to steal;
He sold his broncs to the Army,
Which paid for his next meal.

Then Miss Bad Luck she came again,
That ugly, dirty witch;
She threw a bad bronc at him,
And he ended in a ditch.

Broke of leg and down of soul,
He tried to find his way;
He got healed up, but not quite straight,
And he's limping to this day.

The first broke leg was quite enough
To kill off most young men;
But it was number two and three
That did the cowboy in.

He hunted jobs for a cripple,
For something a hobbler could do,
But the writing was on the bunkhouse wall:
Cowboy life was all he knew.

He found just one kind rancher left,
After searching the country wide;
A kind old man much like himself,
With a merciful heart inside.

Pride could be no option,
For what he had to do;
But he found only pity and sad eyes
From the full-time cowboy crew.

He met his job on equal ground,
This tired old bobwire fence;
He'd worked the range for forty years;
This was his recompense.

Now the wind sings in the sagebrush,
Rusted wire its guitar;
And rain drums on a tin roof,
Where his hat and saddle are.

This wasn't the life he wanted,
And given half a chance,
He'd have his wife and children back,
All working on his ranch.

But a broken cowboy has no choice;
And for sure he's got no sense;
On this range, he'll meet his end,
Riding miles of rusted fence.

The Circle Turns

Picasso was the mighty stud,
Leader of the herd;
Many stallions challenged him—
But victory was his word;
Picasso was the lord of all—
None could claim his band;
And the paint stud ruled undaunted
This Colorado land.

He was king over the mountains,
The water and the trees,
Ruler of the prairies
Commander of the breeze.
Corona was a golden stallion,
Colored like the sun;
He ruled another herd of mares,
And the desert they would run.

He sired a little yellow colt
Whose weak and wobbly knees
Seemed like they would let him fall
Against the slightest breeze.
But that little colt grew tall and strong;
His tail flowed like the river;
He took his share of a warrior's strength
From the hand of Courage-giver.

Sand Wash Basin they called home,
The lair of roving winds;
And here they kept themselves aloof
From all of mankind's sins.
Water ran but scarcely,
Amid juniper and sage;
And Time came here infrequently,
When it wished to turn a page.

The land remained the same here
As two centuries before;
Picasso roamed these badlands;
He never needed more.
One day there came a golden stud
That none had ever seen;
He was large and sleek and wonderful,
His muscles long and lean;

He loped into the valley,
Saw Picasso's band;
His heart began to swiften—
He coveted command;
Week by week he watched the herd,
Waiting for the day
That he could face Picasso
And send him on his way.

It was early of a morning—
The herd had come to feed
Along the shore of a desert lake,
Picasso in the lead;
The palomino stood back in the trees—
His presence was unknown;
But Picasso smelled him on the air

And in the breeze's moan;

So he gazed across the water's swell,
Testing of the air,
Wondering what stallion
Would dare invade his lair.
The call came across the water,
Cold and piercing shrill,
Ominous to Picasso,
Who sensed a deadly chill,

For there was something in that call
That spoke to him the end;
Yet it placed a power in his bones,
And bold strength it did lend.
Then the other horse was there,
A-pawing of the earth,
And Picasso's mares, and his young colts
Were giving him a berth.

Picasso raised his tail high,
Breathed in the other stud;
He stood stock-still and watched him
Gallop through the mud;
And now the two were face to face,
Gazing at their foe,
This young warrior son of Corona,
His head held way down low.

Picasso seemed to understand
The end had come at last;
He found his old mind wandering
Across a glorious past.
He recalled a time when *he* had faced

The leader of the band—
When he had fought and won this herd
And the kingdom of this land;

No good thing lasts forever—
The old horse knew this proof;
The palomino looked intense,
And fierce of tooth and hoof;
The mares and young had turned away,
Then stopped to view the show;
To watch the fight with Picasso
And this wild-eyed palomino.

It was the pinto stallion,
To surprise and pride of all,
Who reared up on his hind hooves,
Screamed and rolled the ball;
He leaped to where the younger one
Stood pawing at the dirt,
Sank his teeth into his neck
And strove to make it hurt;
It *did* hurt, too,
The stud's scream showed;
Picasso watched him tear away,
And victory he crowed.

But the yellow stud was coming back,
Blood lust in his eye;
Picasso couldn't stem this tide,
No matter how he'd try;
The stallions pounded, struck, and bit,
Set the hair a-fly;
Sent great clouds of swirling dust
Up into the sky;

But Picasso fast was weakening,
His trembling limbs they showed
That he could not keep up the fight
And walk the victor's road.
So with a cry, Picasso
Galloped for the hills,
Charging toward the mountains'
Familiar rocks and rills.

He never stopped his traveling,
Till he was far away;
Till he could let his ears escape
His foe's victorious neigh;
And Picasso now had no one
And had lost his mountain home;
So he joined the bachelor mustangs,
For death sought those alone.

And now the young stud,
Warrior, would rule until he found
The stallion mightier than he,
Who'd claim the victor's ground.
Down below, a grassy swale,
Warrior with the herd;
Twelve long years had passed,
When there came the shadow of a bird.

It was the golden eagle,
Guardian of the land,
The mountains and the valleys
That across the desert spanned.
The eagle saw a buckskin stud,
His tail flowing black;
The eagle sensed that Warrior

Was soon to lose the pack.

The mighty sea had reached the shore,
The river had reached its bend;
The day had come that Warrior
Would see a ruler's end;
And so the circle turns and rolls,
The sun will rise and set;
The wind alone tells haunting tales
Of the stallions that have met.

Slim

You've rode your final mustang, Slim;
The winds of change have swept you
Right off the range you called your own
And from the hills that kept you
A free man with a will of iron
And nerves and hands of steel;
You're old now, cowboy;
Now tell me—how's it feel?

Your legs are pretty near stove up—
Your hands are weak and feeble;
You use a box to mount a horse,
For without it you're unable.
There's a wheezing in your aging voice
That scares me half to death;
And my heart dies down inside me
While you fight for every breath.

I don't have your leathery skin
From years of riding fence
When cowboys' hearts were open,
And they lived by common sense;
I don't have your battle scars,
Your hands as tough as gloves;
I ain't seen near the country,
Nor known as many loves.

Cowboy, you're my hero—
You've kept on wild and free;
You weren't all slick and civilized,
Like they wanted you to be.
You made a bed on thorns or rocks,
And that was where you lay,
Listening to ghostly echoes
On the wind at the break of day.

You've looked at wolves through rifle sights,
But you're too much the same;
You let them slip back to the trees
While you searched for other game.
I guess you'd smile to know I knew,
For you thought you had it hid;
But I saw the lonely wolf in you
When I was just a kid.

You couldn't shoot a timber wolf
No more than you would a mustang;
You lay and listened too many nights
To the haunting songs he sang.
Partner, I know there's tears in you
That won't be seen in comp'ny;
They won't be seen, but you can't hide
Them anymore from me.

We're just alike, old pal,
And we're sick about the change;
About the awful "progress"
That has smothered out the range.
We weep to see the cities grow,
To see the sage mown down;
We'd rather die than pack our gear

And move on into town.

I remember you in younger days,
With jingling spurs and leather chaps,
Riding out in spite of your busted arm
Done up with straps.
I recall your sweat-stained cowboy hat,
Your boots with slanted heel;
And most of all the important way
You made a green kid feel.

You roped old Buck from the wild herd
When he was just a colt;
You tamed him, but he always kept
The fire of a lightning bolt.
No other man could ride old Buck—
His only friend was you;
And I guess you never partnered up
With another horse so true.

You've given me an order, friend,
That I cannot ignore;
It must be sore important;
You never ordered me before.
Saddle up old Buck, you say,
And draw the cinch up tight;
And lead him out real patiently,
For old Buck has lost his sight.

I know you love old Buck, my friend,
But a man don't ride blind horses,
Unless they both know real well
Exactly what their course is;
You're riding up to Lookout Point,

Where the cliff it drops off steep,
Into the winding river,
No more than three feet deep.

It's a drop of a hundred feet, I'd guess,
To a bed of glistening stones;
It's just the kind of place
You always said you'd leave your bones.
Slim, I know you know the trail,
But I'm asking if you would
Just let me lead old Buck
At least a couple miles if I could.

I'll sing you "Twilight on the Trail",
And "Teardrops in My Heart";
But my tears won't be in my chest
As I watch you depart.
I'll hum a line of "Last Roundup"
Before my vocals quit me,
Then I'll sit under the lonesome pine
Before real sorrow hits me.

There's a chilly breeze up off the sage
That stirs me to the liver;
It carries scent of mustangs
And the soft song of the river.
I hate to see you go, old friend,
And leave me here alone;
But you won't have to see times change,
For you'll lie beneath the stone.

Broke Bones and High Fees

The rodeo's begun, and now
The flags are going out;
And now a bronc comes twisting forth,
The one they call Old Trout;
I chance to spy up in the stands
A weathered old cowpoke;
He was a top hand years ago,
But now he's just a joke.

Still he wears that battered hat
And spurs he wore back then,
When he too rode in these wild west shows,
And as well as any man.

He rode the wild barebacks,
And the saddle broncs and bulls;
And he was in the money
Though the folks called him a fool.
When he was a lad this old man
Had dreamed of being a cowboy;
This had been his greatest goal
And riding broncs his greatest joy.

And when you have a dream,
And when you're young and stout of heart,
You're on the road to fame right then—

You already got a start.
So this old boy had forked the dough
And rode the rodeo,
And left behind him memories
Of the joys and all the woes.

Still he wears that battered hat
And spurs he wore back then,
When he too rode in these wild west shows
And as well as any man.

Then finally his dream was realized,
And it was mighty fine;
And he was the All Around Cowboy
Of nineteen thirty-nine.
But as I watch this old man now
A tear drops from his eye;
The old man's sixty-three now,
And I know he'd like to die,

So now I start to thinking
That this is all in vain:
Paying cash to bust your bones—
This stuff could drive weak men insane.
Still there's nothing like the feeling
Of a bronc between your knees,
And warm applause makes up somehow
For broke bones and high fees.

Mustang

I am the mustang,
Primeval wanderer of the American West;
From pure stock were my ancestors born;
Now I am born of the wind.

From the Arabian, the Spanish barb,
The Tennessee walker, the Saddlebred,
The Andalusian, the Morgan.
The Spaniard brought my fathers, my mothers,
The American and the Frenchman too.

They were set free, lost or escaped.
Now I run free, of mixed blood,
With my torn flags flying,
From the supple crest of my neck,
From behind me,
My flags of victory,
My flags of glory.
In the high plains wind they toss,
The wind that carries scent to me of such as you.
You are not my master.
I am your equal.
If you capture me and treat me as such,
I will respect you.
In time I may be your partner.
But I will never be your slave.

I am the mustang,
Primeval wanderer of the American West.
From pure stock were my ancestors born.
Now I am born of the wind.

Born of fire and of the flood,
Of thunder and of rain,
And of the lightning that pounds the earth
As my hooves pound that same earth.
Ancient am I, ancient as the wisest stallion,
Yet new as the brightest colt.

Follow me, learn my ways;
In time, you may gain my wisdom,
And the wisdom of my forbears.
And if you listen, if you watch me long enough,
You too may one day be one with the land.
Without me, without my kind,
You will not survive.

I am the mustang.

I am born of the wind.

Mesteño

Americans took the name from old Mexico and called him
"mustang". To those south of the border, he would forever
remain . . . Mesteño—the untamed one.

Mesteño, you were born to run this land!
Mesteño, so savage yet so grand!
Mesteño, some would like to see you dead!
Mesteño, they would paint your desert red.
Mesteño, you are part of history;
Mesteño, high desert mystery.

The Spaniards brought your fathers here
To aid in exploration;
But you found your way into the hands
Of a hundred Indian nations.
You've been the bane of cattlemen,
You brought them stress and strife;
And many a mighty mustang
To a rifle lost his life.

You run the wild prairies far;
You climb the broken mountains;
You'll take your drink from a water hole,
Or from a pristine fountain.
Black and buckskin, bay and roan,
Sorrel and pinto too;

You paint the American West—
Mustang pure and true.

The deserts of Wyoming!
The hills of Idaho!
Montana or Nevada—wherever you may go,
You symbolize our freedom
As you ramble to and fro!

Mesteño, you were born to run this land!
Mesteño, so savage yet so grand!
Mesteño, some would like to see you dead!
Mesteño, they would paint your desert red.
Mesteño, you are part of history;
Mesteño, high desert mystery.

Introduction: The following two poems, like the poem which opens this book and provides its title, probably seem very similar. They are actually a poem version and a song version of the same basic story, the tale of one aging cowboy and his ironic fate on the western range.

Rusted Old Bobwire

I've hated you, you doggone cuss—
You cut apart my range;
You're an ugly scar upon a land
That didn't need no change;
I hate to say this kind of thing—
It tends to tell my age—
But I was here upon this land
When it was only sage.

Hell, I can tell you tales
About a time not long ago
When yonder valley, in the spring,
Was filled with buffalo;
The West was really wild then—
The Indian still roamed;
He camped here in this very spot
In the mountains he called home.

'Course then in came the white man,
And the rest has all been told;
They killed off all those red men,

For their land and for their gold;
But even then, you cussed wire,
The West just wouldn't die;
She had wild oats still left to sow,
And she was ridin' high.

From Texas came the longhorn,
A stout and sturdy breed,
Without borders nowhere on the land
That they must stop and heed;
I was just a young man then,
With a body taut and lean;
I came up with a herd of steers,
Bound for Abilene.

Eight hundred dusty miles, they say,
Without a fence to cross;
And the only thing we'd answer to
Was one cagey trail boss;
Miles and miles of virgin land
Stretched on out before;
Tracts of untrod sagebrush
And grassy hills galore.

I was young, and I was tough,
And my partners then were, too;
We had steel pipes for innards,
And veins that ran cold blue;
Times were hard, and so were we,
And we didn't want to see
The hordes of hungry settlers
From east to Californie.

But even if we closed our eyes

And swore 'twas just the wind,
Like the buffalo gone before 'em,
Them folks kept pouring in;
And pretty soon they wanted all the land
Divided, like back east,
So's all of us cowpunchers
Soon come to know the Beast.

And you're the Beast, you old Bobwire,
You dirty rotten filth—
You snuck across this cattle range
With true, uncanny stealth;
Again I'll say I've cussed you,
Till I had no more breath;
I've seen you rip a cowboy up
And hang a calf to death.

I got a scar across my back
I got because of you,
And I've fought some men who brought you in,
For the damage that you do.
I've seen you rake a leg to bone
On the best darn horse I had,
And you'd a damn shore done the same to me,
But my legs was leather clad.

Now them big old longhorn steers
Just stand and bawl, forlorn;
Like me, they know they ain't
The free critters they was born;
Hell, a man can't ride here anymore,
No more 'n a country mile,
Without he sees you, old Bobwire,
Stretched in dandy style.

I'll say I've rode across the plains
A midnight ride or two
When me and the boys from the old Bar None
Done took the shears to you;
I ain't afraid to say it,
'Cause you made my life a hell,
By invading every valley,
Every mountain, every dell.

There's those who swore to have my blood
For cutting up their fence,
But if they'd a known the hate in me,
They'd've called on better sense;
They'd've let me ride across the range
And make it free again;
They'd've let me and the old Bar None
Go where we had the yen.

For if the truth be known right now, Bobwire,
I'd a shucked a gun or two,
To kill the man who strung you out
'Cross the ranges that we knew;
But it never came to guns for me—
Just my fists that drove men down;
A time or two I knocked
Some dirt-poor farmer to the ground.

I've hated you, you bloody string,
I've took yer name in vain;
And if I had my youth back,
I'd do it all again;
I've cussed at you and called you names
I wouldn't call the devil . . .
But I'll be square with you, Bobwire,

And tell it on the level.

I ain't the boy I used to be,
An' I can't rope a cow,
Can't get up on them ornery broncs—
My bones ain't fit somehow;
Bobwire, I'm all busted up—
My knee's got rheumatiz;
I can't head off one stampeding calf,
And here my problem is:

The boss says he can't use me now
To ride a wild cayuse,
But it just ain't in his honest heart
To go and cut me loose;
He has one more last job for me,
One to see me through,
So I can stay on this old spread,
On the ranges that I knew.

Well, I guess you got me figgered,
Why there's pliers in my hand,
And why I sit a buckboard
When you see me cross this land;
Like you, old boy, I'm rusted up,
And there's parts of me that's broke;
And to all them younger punchers
I ain't nothing but a joke.

But though my pride's been bruised a bit,
There's still a dream inside;
And I hate like hell admitting it,
But my thankfulness I can't hide;
You've given me the only way I had

To stay out on this range,
To try to keep them towns at bay
And fight them winds of change.

I spent my young years tearing you down
And destroying yer posts with fire;
I'll use the rest out where I love,
Mending broken wire;
I've cussed you and I've hated you,
But I guess I'd be a liar
To say I wasn't thankful now for
Rusted old Bobwire.

Bobwire

There's a pall of dust hovering over this plain;
I've been watching the sky, praying for rain;
But it ain't coming—we all know it's true;
Like the free range I love, this cowboy is through.

I came back from the war, looking for home;
But there wasn't one left, and my folks were all gone;
I found me a wild horse, and I tamed him to ride;
Then I left all alone with a gun at my side.

I got lucky, I guess, when I found that old man
Trying to hire a crew of a dozen good hands;
And we bunched up a herd of the wildest kind,
Then we headed them north to the railroad line;

I was a young cowboy, too wild to fit in;
I lived my life horseback with the other tough men;
I lived by the lasso, and sometimes by the gun
I slept on the prairie, and the cities I shunned.

I ate beans for breakfast, and sometimes ate beef;
I've been called a rascal, but never a thief;
And I'm here to tell you I was a top hand;
When I hired with an outfit, I rode for the brand.

When the Big Die-up came, we weren't ready for it;

But I cinched up my tree, and I clamped on the bit;
I had suffered before, and I could do it again;
Least that's what I thought, till the wire came in.

I just wanted a horse with my saddle on him;
If they wanted good hands, come sink or come swim,
I had a stout rope, and my own saddle to boot,
A seat that could ride, and a gun that could shoot.

But it wasn't to be, and the free range dried up;
I was left with my saddle, my gun, and a cup;
But it was empty but for bitter regret
And that damned old grubline was as good as I'd get.

I am an old cowboy, though just fifty-three;
They have a few young hands, and then they have me.
I have torn up the bobwire, from sunup to down;
I have fought any chance of moving to town;
Now they throw it at me: I have only one chance,
And that's why you see me out here riding this fence.
I've hated this bobwire, for it fenced off my West;
Now I'm mending fences, 'cause there ain't nothing left.

So I'm riding this fenceline, a mustang that's broke;
And to all those young cowboys, I am only a joke;
And my worst enemy, the one I fought so hard,
Is this bobwire I string: he's my only pard.

There's a pall of dust hovering over this plain;
I've been watching the sky, praying for rain;
But it ain't coming—we all know it's true;
Like the free range I love, this cowboy is through.

Gringo, Wild Horse

I step out to the old corral,
With its frosted silver rails;
The dawn is come; the sun is nigh,
But there's moon dust on the trails.
The pump runs cold, as thoughts unfold
Of Gringo and years gone by.
And as I watch the horses feed,
The teardrops fill my eyes.

Gringo, wild horse!
Together, we roped the wind.
But those reckless days caught up to us,
Gringo, my Idaho friend.

In the shadows sits your saddle old,
It is worn out, but it never failed;
I rode that seat through dust and snow,
As with me your mighty hooves sailed.
I see the sun put frost to run,
And it trickles down the pole;
There's a missing sight out in the pen,
And in my heart, a hole.

Gringo, wild horse!
Too wild to ever be tamed.
We busted brush, and branded hides,

Gringo, too tough to be lamed.

You were heedless of the danger there,
In those grizzly bear cubs two.
That mother bear, would have killed me dead,
Gringo, if not for you.

The first cub lay beside the trail,
He didn't seem to know fear;
But the second bawled and ran for the trees,
Knowing salvation was near.
On foot I was, to rest your legs,
And you could have high-tailed for home.
Instead, you chose to face that beast,
There on the blue mountain dome.

Gringo, wild horse!
You fought her with all that you had.
You pummeled her with iron hooves,
But Gringo, she busted you bad.
That mama bear could not prevail;
She ran off with pulverized paw.
But you, brave horse, did pay the most,
With that badly shattered jaw.
The blood ran from your leg unchecked,
And I tried to get help for you;
But ere we made the old home ranch,
Your moments on this earth were few.

Gringo, wild horse!
Together we roped the wind.
You saved my life, and gave your own,
Gringo, my Idaho friend.

Your sight grew dim, as I looked on,
Helpless to lend any aid.
I watched the spirit leave your eyes,
As your head, in my lap you laid.
Your breath came hard, you flicked an ear,
Looking up into my eyes.
And I learned then that cowboys cry,
As my best friend said his goodbyes.

Gringo, wild horse!
You've ridden beyond the big bend.
I loved you dear, you foolish horse,
Gringo, my Idaho friend.

MUSINGS

AND

MELANCHOLY

The Empty Saddle of Old Paint

I walk alone to the old corral
And stand there in the dust;
This ranch once made us money,
But now it's just a bust.

A wind comes rustling down,
Shaking dreams out of the trees,
And my memories are riding
On that cool southwestern breeze.

I place a hand on the old top rail—
It's smooth now with the years;
I see a gray horse tail hair,
And I choke back all the tears.

It's caught there on a splinter,
The one rough spot on the rail,
The only thing that's left of Paint—
A hair out of his tail.

There's a saddle hanging rough and rotted,
At the shed that sits nearby;
That tree won't fit no other horse,
No matter how I'd try.

That saddle fit you perfectly,

Just like it was built there
Right over the spotted pattern
Of your pretty pinto hair.

There's a trail up through the jagged pines,
Another on the ridge;
A rough road follows the river,
Then crosses the Bobtail Bridge.

One path leads up high,
Into the snowy mountains;
We found that path ten years ago
That led to Bear Creek's fountains.

There's many trails we've ridden, friend,
And I'd just like to know,
Which is the one you follow,
And where do you like to go?

Where do you ride tonight, Old Paint?
Your rotted saddle's hanging here;
Are there still some trails we missed
That keep you roaming near?

I don't guess there's some cowboy's spirit
Riding you around Heaven,
For no man but me could ride you,
Here on the Diamond Seven.

And as for me, Old Paint,
I spend a lot of my time hiking,
For since you left, my own two hooves
Are just more to my liking.

I've tried to make another friend
Out of a horse like you,
But I just can't seem to find one
That's anywhere near so true.

The song says I should die off first,
And then Paint packs me away;
So it wasn't right that you said good-bye,
And I buried you that day.

Dirty Trick

I took a vicious blow today:
My best friend, Jack, just passed away;
There weren't no way for me to know,
The way of all the world he'd go;
He up and went, without me knowing,
While that cold north wind was blowing.
He left behind a legacy—
Now he is just a memory;
How was I to know my friend would go
And leave me with this awful woe?
He never said a word before,
About approaching Heaven's door.
Now I'm too late, for gone he is;
His spirit up to Heaven riz.
I'd like to have my old pal back;
I miss him sore, my old friend, Jack.
But I guess that Jack's been served;
He went and got what he deserved;
He's gone out of this lonely world,
And for Jack the final flag's unfurled;
He's gone from all the toil and strife,
To make himself a better life.
Well, Jack was old as history—
He was deaf, and he could hardly see;
And me, I ain't too dang much better,
And I curse old Jack—my Irish setter.

Now, friends, I hope that you can see,
It ain't Jack's death that bothers me;
The only thing I really mind
Is he died and left his pal behind.

Introduction: The specifics of my young career in poetry are long-since forgotten, but the one thing I do know for certain is that the following poem, first written in the following, free verse, style, was one of my very first forays into the world of poetry, and certainly my first attempt at free verse.

New Frontier (Unrhymed)

The new age—civilization, they call it;
Progress, too. Progress and improvement.
Innumerable solemn gray skyscrapers
Thrusting up to Heaven.

Technology's A-bombs and rockets,
Rockets that soar far away,
So bridging the gap
Between this civilization and raw frontiers beyond.

Freeways—super highways, some call them;
They thread across the nation, now,
Packed tight with smoke-trailing vehicles.
They run, now, where once the mighty bison ran,
Where the American Indian hunted in order to live.

No place is immune to this "progress," this "improvement."
These super highways have broken the spirit
Of the awesome Rockies,
Torn through the heart and soul of the Mojave,

And Death Valley,
Where once no one wandered but the brave.

But Henry Ford, and others of his mold
Changed all that.
They replaced the simple horse-drawn buggies
With their fast-moving, invincible metal monsters.

Nowhere to go now but you see
The metallic sheen of these beasts
As they scream their way up
Mighty hills of brush and rock.

The trails of Jeeps and motorbikes
Criss-cross these hills now,
Where once would have run
The paths of the deer and bighorn sheep.

The era of the Indian and mountain man saw its end;
Over a century ago it died, when already
Civilization had traversed where
No one had guessed it had the ability to.

In came the cowboy, the American hero,
The enduring, everlasting survivor;
The Indian sadly called that civilization.
If they had only seen;
The heroic era of the cowboy, too, saw its end
With that of the century.

Then came the 1920's, the 30's, the 40's and 50's
With all their progress.
The 60's pretended man on the moon, a shock to all;
No place to be alone now.

The shores of river and ocean are crowded;
The mighty gas machines carry men far back now,
Where before only the sturdiest of creatures could go.

Yes, they call this civilization.
Then call it what they like, I say,
Civilization, progress, or improvement.
But once there was a time when neighbor trusted neighbor,
And "neighbor" meant friend.

One could leave an unlocked house,
Coming back weeks later to find all intact.
I say, take this civilization—carry it away.
As for me, I will take the civilization of
The mountain man or the cowboy.

They can keep their new frontier.

Introduction: I wrote the following poem, intermixed with pieces of famous "Western" music, when I was at the height of my Cowboy Poetry "career", if such it can be called. Sadly, as the complete poem/song took over thirteen minutes to get through, I never completed the task of memorizing it, and this one was never performed on the stage . . .

Medley of the West

"As I walked out on the streets of Laredo,
As I walked out in Laredo one day,
I spied a poor cowboy, wrapped up in white linen,
Wrapped up in white linen, as cold as the clay . . . "

I was drifting down in Idaho,
After summering in Montan',
Feeling near as lonesome
As any cowboy can.
The West was changing quickly—
I could see it every day,
So I sang to myself in the saddle,
To push all my sadness away.

"I ride an old Paint; I lead an old Dan.
I'm going to Montana, to throw the hooley-ann;
They feed in the coulee, they water in the draw,
Their tails are all matted, their backs are all raw.
Ride around, little dogies, ride around them slow,

For the fiery and the snuffy are rarin' to go."

I saw the old man toward evening,
At a spread that had seen better days;
Whiling away his hours
In the gathering evening haze.
He sat upon his front porch
As the sun bled from the sky,
Staring toward the Sawtooths
With a faraway look in his eye.
He held a faded guitar—
His only company,
And he was singing a song,
As if to welcome me.

"The cattle are prowlin', the coyotes are howlin',
Way out where the dogies bawl.
Where spurs are a-jinglin', a cowboy is singin'
His lonesome cattle call.
Ooh, ooh, oo-oo-oo. . . . Singin' his cattle call."

I was traveling hungry,
And needing a soft, warm bed;
I rode my old buckskin across the yard
Of the run-down old homestead.
The old man looked up and saw me,
And without even skipping a beat,
He changed to a song that made me smile,
With a melody jaunty and sweet.

"As I was out ridin' one mornin' for pleasure
I spied a cowpuncher a-ridin' along.
His hat was thrown back, and his spurs were a-jinglin',
And as he approached, he was singin' this song:

Whoopie-ti-yi-yo, git along, little dogies,
It's your misfortune and none of my own;
Whoopie-ti-yi-yo, git along, little dogies,
You know that Wyomin' will be your new home."

His gray hair was a-thinning—
There were wrinkles on his brow;
Gone was the spryness of youth,
Replaced by gnarled limbs now.
But he stood up gamely to meet me,
With a sparkle of mirth in his eye;
"Rest a spell, stranger—you're welcome."
Then he turned to the door with a sigh.
I climbed down from my buckskin
And ground-tied him near a trough,
Then took another moment
To drag the saddle off.

The man had cooked some supper,
And we sat to it there in the gloom,
Eating in silence and darkness,
As if in the throat of a tomb.
The wind began to whistle
Around the cabin door,
And he put a match to a lantern,
Sending its light 'cross the floor.

Then he reached for his guitar, saying,
"I hope that you like a rough tune.
For I guess I've grown accustomed
To singin' my songs to the moon."
He hefted the long-necked guitar
With a thin leather strap for his neck,
And the scratches on that old guitar

Told of at least one good wreck.
Where his fingers pressed down there were craters,
Worn in the wood over years;
And the blotchy dark marks on top of the thing
I fancied were left there by tears.

"I used to be a cowboy, like you,
If I figure you right.
And I rode the grub line and begged for a meal
On many a long, lonely night.
I'll tell you the tales if you'll listen,
Though this guitar's all faded and cracked;
It's been through the mill, I guess you can tell;
It's my best friend, and son, that's a fact."

He leaned back a mite in his rocker,
And boys, I am right here to tell it,
He started to sing, and that old worn-out voice,
Well, that night it sounded like velvet.

"I'm lonesome but happy, rich but I'm broke,
And the good Lord knows the reason: I'm just a cowpoke.
From Cheyenne to Douglas, all the ranges I know;
'Cause I drift with the wind, no one cares where I go.
Oo--oo-oo, oo-oo-oo--oo-oo. . . ."

He spoke of his days on the prairie,
Where the wind whipped his young features red,
Where he played that guitar for all of the boys,
Who now, rest their souls, were all dead.
He spoke of a horse he had ridden—
A level, smooth-riding old bay;
He had to shoot it when it busted a leg,
And he mourned for that horse to that day.

"Ole Faithful, we roamed the range together;
Ole Faithful, in every kind of weather.
When your roundup days are over,
There'll be pastures white with clover,
For you, Ole Faithful, pal of mine."

I lowered my head when he finished,
For that song saddened me to the core;
I hated to think what would happen
When Old Buck wasn't with me no more.
But just when my sorrow was deepest,
He started a glad melody,
And my thoughts lifted up, as he gave me a smile,
And started to sing cheerfully:

"I got a hundred and sixty acres in the valley,
Got a hundred and sixty million stars above.
Got an old bay hoss, I'm the guy who's boss,
On the hundred and sixty acres that I love."

Then the old man returned melancholy,
Singing of romance and love,
And the girl who he cherished until she left him
And roamed to her mansion above.

"When it's springtime in the Rockies, I'll be coming back to you,
Little sweetheart of the mountains with your bonnie eyes of blue.
Once again, I'll say I love you as the birds sing all the day.
When it's springtime in the Rockies, in the Rockies far away."

Then he spoke of the dying of cowboys,
And of ranches long gone by the way,
Of the days long ago, when a man would be happy,
To work all day long for his pay.

"The wheel of the wagon is broken;
It ain't gonna turn no more.
My days on the prairie are over;
There's weeds 'round the old ranch door.
There ain't any campfire a-smokin',
Where we sang when the day was through,
The wheel of the wagon is broken,
And gone is the west I knew."

He told me his fingers were tired;
He guessed he'd played on way too long;
But before he lay down, he wanted to leave me
His favorite old cowboy song.
He looked right at me and he smiled,
His eyes flanked by jagged crow's feet;
"Mister, I know I am goin' to Heaven,
All of my old friends to meet."

"When it's twilight on the trail, and my voice is still
Please plant this heart of mine underneath the lonesome pine on
the hill."

I rode out of there that next morning,
With a lonely fresh grave on the hill,
Beneath the old pine, where the crooked creek winds,
And the old cowboy's guitar lies still.
When the tears had all dried from my whiskers,
I turned in the saddle to gaze,
Across rolling sage that had seen many cowboys,
Way back before civilized days.

There was only one tune in my mind then,
But I just couldn't sing it out loud;
So I remained voiceless, and the old man's ghost sang,

While I only listened, head bowed.

"I'm headin for the last roundup.
To the faraway ranch of the boss in the sky.
Where the strays are counted and branded, there go I.
I'm headed for the last roundup.
Get along, little dogie, get along,
Get along, get along, little dogie, get along.
Get along, little dogie, get along,
Get along, get along, little dogie, get along.
I'm headin' for the last roundup.
Get along, little dogie, get along."

The Grave of Indian Bill

There's a spot above the valley,
Where grass grows on the hill,
Where the wind blows cold and bittersweet
On the grave of Indian Bill.

He was half Shoshone—
His dad had come from Maine
Before the Great War swept the land
And brave men died in vain.

No man stood as proud and tall,
So straight of back and limb,
Nor had the crowd of youngsters
That nearly worshiped him.

Bill, he was a pure man,
Clean of heart and soul;
Never a man he cheated,
Never a thing he stole.

I was the man who brought him in
That tragic day he died,
And out of a crowd of hardened men
I'm the only one who cried.

Young Ben Sharp was hunting elk

When his horse it went plumb wild;
It bucked and flung him in the air,
And onto his back he was piled.

It was cold and snowy on the hill,
And Ben was all alone;
When my friend Indian Bill arrived,
Ben Sharp was cold as stone.

Indian Bill did the best he could
To bring the young man in,
But a blizzard welled up from the north,
And the clothes he wore were thin.

He had to leave young Ben Sharp there
And get out of the storm;
He took his horse to get to town,
His coat to keep him warm.

He headed to town to get some help,
Someone to come for Ben;
He needed a hand to bury him
Down in some sheltered glen.

The Murphy boys were riding out,
In search of a wayward cow;
Indian Bill had found it first,
And was bringing it in to them now.

But they came upon Bill on the trail to town,
Young Ben Sharp's horse beneath;
And with their cow in front of him,
They knew he was a thief.

It didn't matter what Bill said,
The Murphys believed not a word;
Indian Bill, he was no good,
In spite of the things they had heard.

If Ben was dead, as he surely was,
It hadn't been done by mistake;
Surely Bill had killed him
For the buckskin horse and a stake.

So they tied his hands and they led his horse
To a lonesome old fir on the hill;
They were dead sure convinced that Bill had stole,
For an Indian always will.

Indian Bill was a brave young man,
And he would not beg or plead;
He told them simply how he came by the cow,
How he came by the buckskin steed.

But the Murphy boys were fired up,
And for Bill there was no last request;
His body swung against the stiff breeze
When died the last light in the west.

I found my friend Bill in the morning,
And I had to get him to town;
I cried o'er his stiff hanging body,
And I cut my poor friend down.

And in Ben Sharp's coat pocket, I found a small note;
The words, they were dim, but I read:
"I'm in a bad way, my sweet Mary,
And fear that I soon will be dead.

If anyone finds this here message,
Please take it to her so she'll know,
And take this old pony—it's all that I have—
And lay me out here in the snow."

The note was signed by young Ben Sharp,
Signed in a shaky hand;
It told me a tale as true as my friend,
Of his ever-honest brand.

Well, Indian Bill, I reckon you're gone;
You lie on the hill where it's steep;
And I pray that your God will comfort you,
Deep in the ground where you sleep.

54

Introduction: At around fifteen years of age, my mother introduced me to the music of a man who would go on to become one of the greatest heroes of my lifetime, a man I later met, along with all his family at his home, and who treated me like his brother and friend. These two pieces are actually songs, rather than poems, but without music on the page I challenge you to know the difference! R.I.P., Chris LeDoux, 1976 Bareback Bronc riding champion of the world.

Chris Ledoux's Ghost

Sing me your songs of Wyoming,
Powder River, the sand and the sage;
Riding free as the wind on your old buckskin steed,
Sing me your songs of the range.

Tell me your tales of a cowboy
Driving hard just to make the next show;
Your stories made me taste the dust in my teeth
Riding broncs at the big rodeo.

And you're still out there riding the prairie,
I can see you as you crest the hill,
And Chris LeDoux's ghost lives in this guitar,
And there's no doubt that he always will.

I remember that boy and his gui-tar,
A shy kid just fourteen years old

Your "Caballo Diablo" sent chills up my spine,
And I knew then that I had struck gold.

You taught me to get back up on 'em,
If ever I got thrown from my star,
And Chris LeDoux will ride on in my heart,
For his ghost lives here in my guitar.

And you're still out there riding the prairie,
I can see you as you crest the hill,
And Chris LeDoux's ghost lives in this guitar,
I promise that you always will.

"Good Enough for Country"

Out in old Wyoming,
Where they call sagebrush a tree;
I met my hero, Chris LeDoux,
Out on his property.
We talked of life, and rodeo;
Then went out to my car;
Chris had asked to play some songs
On my battered old guitar.

He admired that Harmony Master;
He liked the tone it had;
That old guitar had seen a lot
In travels with my dad.
He tuned my guitar up,
And when it sounded fine to me;
Chris grinned at me and said these words:
"It's good enough for country."

Good enough for country!
My hero said to me.
Good enough for country,
And to strum a melody.
Good enough for country?
Well you can plainly see,
"Good enough for country"
Is good enough for me.

He played on my old guitar
Some songs that touched my soul;
I played some of my own songs,
And he played some rock and roll.
The sun was sinking low by then,
And it was time to go.
The time was near to say goodbye
And head on down the road.

That cowboy had his photo
Taken standing next to me;
We spoke a while longer,
Then parted company.
The afternoon I spent with him
Will live on in my soul;
Chris has gone to heaven now
To ride their rodeo.

Good enough for country!
My hero said to me.
Good enough for country,
And to strum a melody.
Good enough for country?
Well you can plainly see,
"Good enough for country"
Is good enough for me.

And good enough for Chris LeDoux
Is good enough for me.

Don't Give Your Hand to a Soldier

I was done, going home,
Recalling all those years ago I'd left to roam,
And my girl, and the war,
And all the memories gone before;
And I cried to think she left me,
And I tried to understand
Why my girl wouldn't give to me her hand.
But I found the reasons by and by,
When I was packed and gone:
Her dad had said, "Don't give your life to Tom."

Don't give your hand to a soldier,
A young man dressed in green;
He'll lead you straight through hell, my girl,
A hell that you ain't seen;
And when you think he's coming home,
His term is nearly done,
You'll hear your young man's fallen by the gun.

So I'm home, home again;
I left a boy but come back now a man;
They tell me Katie met a man,
And she gave to him her hand.
And they went away together,
To a place so far away
And Mama reads the news she got today;

Her man had died in a fiery crash;
The highway claimed his life;
It weren't no gun that widowed that man's wife.

So don't give your hand to a stranger,
A young man tall and lean,
He'll lead you straight through hell, my girl,
A hell you've never dreamed;
Just when you think he's coming home,
His traveling's nearly through,
You hear your man's not coming home to you.

The Eyes of Your Heart

You're feeling lost and lonely;
You have nowhere to turn;
The trials of life are weighing you down heavy.
You have no one to reach for,
And life is closing in;
You're passing through a storm, and you're not ready.

Get on your feet and try to do your part;
Sometimes when you're feeling lost,
You just have to make a start,
And see God's world through the eyes of your heart.

That old man sitting near you
Could be your greatest friend.
He's been alive so long and he's still smiling;
Reach out to him and listen;
And don't just shut him out;
He's fought hard truths while never reconciling.

Get on your feet and try to do your part;
Sometimes when you're feeling lost,
You just have to make a start,
And see God's world through the eyes of your heart.

You can make life just as easy as you please
Or make it all too difficult to bear;

You can walk a muddy, rutted path of anger and despair,
Or walk softly and seek beauty everywhere.

See the colors of the rainbow,
And watch the evening sky,
Look for glory in the morning sun that streams;
A glorious home is waiting,
For those who do their best,
So reach inside yourself, and strive to find your dreams.

Get on your feet and try to do your part;
Sometimes when you're feeling lost,
You just have to make a start,
And see God's world through the eyes of your heart.

Fade Away with the Moon

I stare at the dark, while I wait for the day;
You lie close beside me yet planets away;
The stars are like diamonds that vanish with dawn;
And then, like our love . . . they're gone.

The coyotes are wailing, and the owls cry out too;
I mimic them both, crying for you;
The moon has a sad face while watching you sleep;
Feeling my sorrow . . . so deep.

I still make believe in these shadows so dark
That you want me and need me, and I have your heart;
The night, she is kind, but I fear for the day;
The sunshine it steals . . . you away.

I always find hope in the dark;
Is there still love, if only a spark?
I always find love, promised by the moon,
But the night, she is going, and the day comes too soon.

These shadows hide truth, and they do it so well;
They make me feel heaven as I'm heading for hell;
A soft breeze it cools me and makes my world feel right;
But the tragic truth waits . . . in the light.

The stars glitter on, while beside me you sleep;

Our love seems unchanging, in this silence so deep;
I pray, and I cry, and I wish it away,
But the fickle night soon . . . becomes day.

I always find hope in the dark;
Is there still love, if only a spark?
I always find love, promised by the moon,
But the night, she is going, and the day comes too soon.

Silver hope it shines on in the dark;
Brightness and beauty, alive in love's spark;
I know you must leave me, and you'll be gone soon;
You'll leave me tomorrow—and fade away with the moon.

Riches

I may be old and gray,
But there's wisdom in my eyes;
Wisdom gained from trying things
That cut me down to size.

I started out this life with dreams
Of being famous and rich,
And knew if I hunted long enough
That I would find a niche.

Where'd they go, those dreams?
Did they set outside and rust?
Or did they fall beneath my feet,
And get trampled into dust?

I'm old now, and gray as death,
As I told you once before,
And riches, fame, and glory?
I don't even care no more.

My riches come from sitting a horse,
And gazing over this land,
Seeing that humble cabin
That I built with my two hands.

My fame comes from the friends of mine,

Those of them who're left,
And the spirit of my woman,
Who left me quite bereft.

I've viewed the foolish whims of youth,
And I have the Lord to thank,
For teaching me the important wealth
Isn't kept within a bank.

It's out there on the land,
And in the folks you've helped along,
It's in the whispering river,
And the meadowlark's sweet song.

It's in the timber, smelling sweet,
That grows up on the hill,
And knowing God watches out for me
And that He always will.

Final Roundup (My Streets of Gold)

There's a valley, down below this hill;
Way up on top, I sit here still;
Horizon-wide is empty space,
But the world is coming to take this place.

I'm just a cowboy, and I don't know
Much about life in those towns below;
I only know it's closing in:
This thing called progress, brought on by men.

And I'm crying deep inside my heart;
It's all changing,
And I've played my part—
Progress is coming, and I rue the day;
This tired old cowboy needs to fade away.

My old cow horse, he stands by me;
It's been this way through history;
But I see a time—this'll all be gone;
Progress is coming, and it won't be long.

But I'm just a cowboy, doing what I know;
Running away from those towns down below;
I guess that I've used up my time;
There's nothing left for me—only the cryin'.

And so I'm crying deep inside my heart;
It's all changing,
And I've played my part—
Progress is coming, and I rue the day;
This tired old cowboy needs to fade away.

But I am praying when all's said and done,
Some other place, beyond the sun;
I'll find a roundup, like the days of old;
And that, my friends, is my streets of gold.

But right now I'm crying deep inside my heart;
This world is changing,
And I've played my part—
Progress is coming, and I rue the day;
This tired old cowboy needs to fade away.

Beyond the far horizon, so I've been told,
I'll find that roundup, my streets of gold.

The Homecoming

He's a rover, a drifter, a wanderer—
He dreams of a faraway land.
Is it travel, danger, adventure?
Well, then he'll try his hand.
He left his wife and children—
Not man enough for that test.
Now he cries when he ponders on them,
But he keeps on riding west.

He works for a year as a miner
Before prospecting on his own;
He rides old Buck, till he's seen better days,
Then trades him in for a roan.
He sinks to his lowest, half starved to death,
And robs a bank in Cheyenne,
Turning to the owl-hoot trail,
To become a wanted man.

But no one knows his name or his face,
And the blue roan takes him far;
In Phoenix he tries the other side,
And there he wears a star.
Then he wanders again, to old Mexico,
Till a *borracho* pulls a knife;
And he has to leave for the border,
After he takes the man's life.

He breaks a rough string
For a rancho on the Rio Santa Cruz;
But he spends his pay in Tucson,
On Monte, Faro, and booze.
So he takes a herd up the trail,
From Austin to Abilene,
And they pay him a hundred dollars,
But the trail's end robs him clean.

And then a ghost passes over him—
His memory of Illinois;
He thinks of his loving Bonnie,
And his daughters, and the boy.
He's been away so long,
He can't even remember their eyes;
And he pictures only blurred faces,
No matter how hard he tries.

He can't go back, but he has to—
Back to the children and wife;
He knows he's already wasted
The best of a fortunate life.
He finds them there waiting for him,
And he knows they always will—
There in the ground where they laid them,
On top of the wind-blown hill.

The Back That Wasn't Turned

I'm a cattleman, born and bred,
I've wished all sheep to wind up dead.
I've spent my life out on the range—
I've lived to see it change.

Them stubble-jumpers eat the grass
Down to the roots wherever they pass.
They turn the range all into chaff;
What they leave won't feed a calf.

And the herders, too, without a doubt,
I'd've opened this country and thrown them out.
They speak Basque or French or often Spanish—
Every tongue, it seems, but English.

Well, I talk harsh, but it ain't real;
I'll tell you how I really feel.
I'm a cowboy—there's no doubt,
But here today the truth will out.

I was lost up in the high country,
In a blizzard so thick I couldn't see;
There wasn't a shred of hope for me
When I fell beneath that tree.

Then I heard a voice—Basque or French,

A sheepman, by the sound an' stench;
He knew my callin', by chaps an' spurs—
The man called off his curs.

They wagged their tails and licked my face,
For a real cowboy a true disgrace;
Then that man gave all his wealth
To nurse me back to health.

His wealth weren't much, I must admit,
But he gave me every bit of it:
His wine, his food, his blanket warm;
He kept me safe from harm.

He didn't have to, but he did;
If he hated me he kept it hid;
I know I'd choused his sheep before—
Thrown a slug at one or more.

He knew it, too, but he took me in,
Knowing it would be a sin
To leave me out there in the snow
Where freezing north winds blow.

So now when I ride out on the range,
My former ways have seen a change.
Not just t'ward him, but all those fellers
That made me froth and beller.

I got a new outlook, my friend,
And a respect for sheepmen that won't end.
My gratitude's forever earned
By a back that wasn't turned.

Justice

The snow drifts gently to the ground,
Goose feathers by the millions, gliding down;
I gaze across the valley floor
But soon won't see it anymore,
For that storm is threatening to drift us in—
In one of the sorrier places I've been.
Up around eight thousand feet,
Where the warmest rain comes down as sleet.

My old horse, Bob, is trusting me
To snatch him from eternity.
But he don't know I'm lost as heck,
And to me he shouldn't trust his neck.
The sad fact is, that I'm likewise—
Praying and trusting in Old Bob's eyes
To get me off this mountainside
Where many a man's laid down and died.

The snow fell softly for a while,
But now slants down in norther style;
I tug the scarf around my ears,
And try to calm my horse's fears;
But he's a horse, and they know best
When the man on top can't pass the test.
Bob, he knows I'm failing him—
I went too far out on the limb.

And now I guess we won't go home;
The ranges of Heaven tomorrow we'll roam;
The snow is ice, the sky is dreary,
And good old Bob is growing weary;
He stumbles and nigh falls down the canyon—
As I my final hopes abandon
For getting back to the old home spread
And resting my bones in my woman's bed.

I've about run out my final string
When my frozen mind thinks an awful thing:
A fellow told me, years ago,
That he once got caught out in the snow;
It whistled up—a real blizzard—
And he froze up to his neck and gizzard;
The only way out, he told himself,
Was to kill his horse, for his own health.

So he shot his horse right in the head,
And cut him open when he was dead;
Then he crawled inside to help keep warm,
And the blizzard winds did no more harm;
But I just can't kill my old friend, Bob;
And him of life I cannot rob.
Besides, that story ain't all done—
And I'll go on, but not for fun:

The man who told that tale to me
Was bound to a wheelchair permanently,
For when that awful storm passed by,
He was froze in his horse, and although he'd try
To free himself, he couldn't make it,
And his limbs were so cold they couldn't take it;
Well, by the time they found that poor young man,

He was stuck like a salmon in a can.

They got him free of his horse, all right,
But the doctor cut off his legs that night;
So I entertain not even a thought
Of crawling in my horse, no matter how hot
It might be inside him when the wind blows cold--
I'd rather stay outside and watch the storm unfold.
And then, my friends, just when I weaken,
I look through the snow and see a beacon.

It's my home lights shining bright for me,
And the big house silhouette I can see!
Well, I'm glad Old Bob I didn't kill,
For 'twas me that took him on the hill.
Bob had sense enough at dawn
To stay inside, but I prodded him on.
So if there's justice on earth at all,
It oughtta be this cowboy taking the fall.

And if someone had a reason to have died,
I should have killed myself and let Bob crawl inside.

Banks of the Yellowstone

It was a simple place, but her grandpa built it right,
Out of hand-hewn logs, stood up straight and sealed tight;
It wasn't much to see, but she had always called it home,
That little log-built house on the banks of the Yellowstone.

I had itchy feet, and I had to see the world;
She thought she'd roped me—she thought she was my girl;
But I had big dreams, and a great big world to roam,
So I left her there on the banks of the Yellowstone.

The calming waters, and that porch there in the shade
A cobalt oil lamp, and that rag rug she had made;
Rising mountains, and waving grass of woven gold,
Were the treasures that her heart would always hold.
She was waiting there where I'd left her all alone,
Weeping by herself on the banks of the Yellowstone.

Now I've seen the world—it wasn't all I hoped to see;
It was a lonely place, fine for some, but not for me;
Now I'm running back, back to the place that she calls home,
Where she waits for me on the banks of the Yellowstone.

Too long I've left her, too long I've been away,
To the islands, where I watched the palm trees sway;
To the Swiss Alps, and the plains of Africa;
Down to old Mexico, and to South America.

Now I'm back here, where the peaceful waters rush,
To the mountains, and the still of winter's hush,
Where the elk herds roam, white swans swim, and otters play,
Looking for my girl, for too long I've been away.
But I've found her, with a man I've never known,
And their two children, on the banks of the Yellowstone.

The man she waits for now is some stranger I don't know,
Who comes back to her, in the peaceful ev'ning glow;
She is waiting for the one who shares her home,
Waiting for some other man on the banks of the Yellowstone.

Waiting for her man on the banks of the Yellowstone.

Born to be a Cowboy

Born—with a rope in my hand;
Born—in a wild, untamed land;
Born and raised atop a horse,
Master of the .44,
Lived my whole life out of doors,
Fightin' wolves and wild boars;
It all ain't so, but it should be;
A cowboy, that is me!

I was born to be a cowboy, something you can see;
I've lived a wild, reckless life, trying to stay free;
Montana is a home to me, riding is my joy;
So you all can see that I was born to be a cowboy.

Morn—rolling out of my bed;
Morn—put a Stetson on my head;
Pulling on my Levi's jeans,
Growing long and lanky lean;
Feeling good but looking mean,
The roughest cowboy ever seen;
I ride the range all day and night;
I think I'm living right.

I was born to be a cowboy, something you can see;
I've lived a wild, reckless life, trying to stay free;
Montana is a home to me, riding is my joy;

So you all can see that I was born to be a cowboy.

Torn—over marrying my girl;
Torn—over leaving my whole world;
I've lived in these hills all my life;
Leaving them cuts like a knife;
Bound for years of city strife,
If she is to be my wife;
I've changed my mind, hon, I can't leave;
I need a life that's free.

'Cause I was born to be a cowboy, something you can see;
I've lived a wild, reckless life, trying to stay free;
Montana is a home to me, riding is my joy,
So you all can see that I was born to be a cowboy.

The Belle of the Ball

The dance started out oh so slowly;
Then you caught my eye at the wall;
And I was a cowboy so lowly,
While you were the belle of the ball.

I knew that I didn't deserve you,
That I was just wasting your time,
But my heart I couldn't hold on to;
It disappeared in that moment sublime.

The angels they brought you down to me,
Out of the blue sky above,
And you shot love's arrow right through me
When you chose this old cowboy to love.

Warmly the bright candles guttered,
To light up the straw on the floor;
"I'd like to dance with you," I stuttered,
"If you'll be seen with a cowboy so poor."

The warm smile on your lips was heaven,
The fire from your blue eyes divine;
And the cowboys out on the Bar Seven,
Would never believe you are mine.

Now the fire in our cabin is gleaming,

As you lie here beside me tonight
And sometimes I think I'm still dreaming,
As I look at your smile so bright.

Now my little sweetheart, I love you,
And I'm so glad you answered my call,
And I'd hold no other woman above you,
For you are the belle of the ball.

Introduction: Michael, whose last name will remain anonymous, came to me in 2020, lonely, broken, and looking for a home. His wife and eleven-year-old daughter, back in his home country of Ireland, had been killed by a drunk driver, and his mind never recovered. Only thirty-seven years of age, he had the look of a man twice that old, and the only place I ever could find youth in him was in his haunted deep brown eyes. I took Michael down to the train yard the last day because even at our house he was still tortured by the memory of the loss of his wife and daughter, and he found once more that "riding" was his only true medicine. I reckon Michael is out there somewhere now, riding . . .

The Rider

I hear the mighty whistle blowing
As the big freight train is rumbling;
As the wild storm approaches,
I can hear the thunder grumbling;
There's a rider somewhere on that train,
Doing well to stay out of the rain;
And the rider he is riding,
For a broken heart he's hiding,
And his time to die he's biding,
So he rides! He rides!

I don't know where he's going,
But I do know how he'll get there;
He'll be riding on a big freight train,

A train that's going nowhere;
He tries to stop and stay somewhere,
But he can't find any comfort there.
So the rider keeps on riding,
While a broken heart he's hiding,
And his time to die he's biding,
So he rides! He rides!

He told me that a drunkard,
Back in far off Ireland
Took this wife and daughter from him,
And they laid them underground;
So now he tries to flee his past,
And his youth is flying by so fast,
But the rider keeps on riding,
For a broken heart he's hiding,
And his time to die he's biding, while he rides. He rides!

The rider he is riding
To his final destination,
Till he's covered every state and town
Across this great big nation;
But he knows he'll never find true peace,
And he will never find release,
Until he draws his final breath
And reaches termination.
So the rider keeps on riding,
And that broken heart keeps hiding,
While his time to die he's biding, and he rides!
And he rides! He rides. He rides!

Introduction: Around the year 2000, I attended a Shoshone-Bannock sun dance on the Sho-Ban reservation. I was so struck with the sights and smells and the whole feel of this ceremony that I came back to work and put this short poem on paper . . .

Sun Dance

Sun dance.

Sun dance has called them here,
Called them to talk to their spirits.

In blankets they sit.
They sit facing east,
Voices hushed, reverent for the break of day.

Sacred dust beneath them,
The sky is gray with dawn,
But in the east, beyond the mountain,
Earth Mother smiles up at strands of pink.

They are the True People,
Come here to cleanse their spirits;
Come here to talk to their spirits;
Come here for the smoke of cedar,
To feel the power of the sun.

84

Introduction: This one frankly probably doesn't need much of an introduction to be powerful, but I will offer one all the same. On the morning of September 11, 2001, I was heading to work at a new fire station from normal, Station 3. Halfway to the station, I turned on the radio and caught strange words, spoken in a strange tone. The story began to unfold that a jet plane had struck one of the Twin Towers, in New York City. About this time, a gut problem hit me that may or may not have been a direct cause of this news. Either way, by the time I arrived at the station, I could only rush past a cluster of two crews of firefighters who were glued to the television in the day room. When I returned, much recovered, it was only to see the horrific sight of not just the one, but both towers vomiting out huge clouds of jet-black smoke and flames. I was immediately moved back to my home station, and shortly after reaching it I watched in horror as the first tower, full of firefighters and policemen, fell to the ground, to the shock of all but those who had done it. Feeling still sick, I went home for most of the day, but upon my return to work in the evening I wrote this poem . . .

A Tear Fell

A tear fell, and was heard around the world.
Morning broke, bright and clear.
A new day, full of hope, full of promise.
Fathers, mothers, sons, daughters—
Family. They kissed, they hugged, they said goodbye.
They would meet again,
When the duties of the day were fulfilled.

Then a tear fell, and was heard around the world.
The unspeakable came to America,
Land of the Free.
Human-filled missiles, balls of fire from the sky.
Twin towers. World icons. Now ominous infernos.
Open mouths, stares of disbelief.
In a moment, the towers were gone.

A tear fell, and was heard around the world.
Piles of rubble remained where hours before
Thousands appeared for a normal day of toil.
Dads, moms, sons and daughters—
If they had not said goodbye, they never would.
Gone in a moment, gone in horror, hurled to their deaths.
America rallied. More important, the World rallied.

A tear fell, and was heard around the world.
Rescuers by the hundreds died

When the behemoths came down.
The hopeless, the helpless, jumped to their deaths,
Hundreds of feet in the air, plummeting like birds,
Forgotten how to fly.
But they will not truly be forgotten.

A tear fell, and was heard around the world.
Broken bodies, broken homes, broken dreams.
The cries of those buried alive went unheard.
But some, by the mercy of God, were saved.
Somehow their angels found them,
Hovering there, weeping, praying.
Calling on that very God their nation had forgotten.

People died that autumn day.
People died by the hundreds.
Defenseless people died without warning.
From the air, they died. From the towers, they died.
They came to rescue their fellow man, and they died.
A monument will rise there, on hallowed ground,
For a tear fell, and it was heard around the world.

—September 11, 2001

Introduction: At the end of September of 2001, after terrorists took down two of our world's icons, tourism in our country, in large part, died. What was tragic to New York City, and indeed our entire free, Christian world, was a boon for intrepid travelers, for it was one of the quietest tourist seasons seen in many years. Yellowstone National Park was more than ever like a piece of heaven. From that trip came this poem . . .

Top of the World

I traveled to the top of the world,
Where eternity unfurled.
Yet time stood still, and always will,
Up at the top of the world.

The wind made the only song,
Cold as it whisked along.
Glaciers bold guarded tales untold,
Far from the hurrying throng.

Nothing moves at the top of the world,
Where the granite is pink and purled.
I felt God there, in the flawless air,
Up at the top of the world.

Bear Tooth Pass. Have you been there?
It rainbows over the top of the world.
Conceived in timber—acres of it. Miles of it.
Timber deep green and flecked

With aspen's gold and sumac's red.

The silent road wends up toward forgotten,
Forbidden, silent castles in stone.
Bear Tooth Pass. Magnificence floods the name
Yet does this place no justice.
Glacial lakes, silent, still, nourish the roots
Of stunted pine and fir.

Spruce that any place else would be king
Here is humbled to earth.
Knuckles and fists of stone lie heaped,
Silently guarding their secrets.
Granite as old as the world.

The summit—God lives here.
You can feel him in every sigh of the wind,
In the flinty soil that scars your feet.
You can see him in the magnificence of the sky,
Where the world begins, and where it ends.

I sit in stunned silence, here at the top of the world,
At the edge of the world.
Below me lie glaciers, trapped in the side of mountains
That plummet out from under me.
Glaciers dirtied by days and weeks, months . . .
Maybe years of summers.
Or was it only an hour?

Below sprawl glacial lakes,
And the contemplation of their cold alone makes me ache.
Lakes as old as the world,
As deep as history.
In the sun they sparkle royal blue, emerald green,

Like a mallard's head, glinting against the sun.

I stare at the vastness.
The unending monumentality of this space in the world,
This space out of the world.
The mind cannot take it in.
To grasp it is a conquest reserved for Gods.

Silence. Silence so all-encompassing it hurts . . .
Yet so complete it heals.
And then the wind—the moaning, rushing wind.
The voices of all the angels of eternity together . . . singing.

Up here on top, only the grass holds turf in place.
The trees, the bravest and highest of them,
Lie far below, stunted, ragged, twisted and bent by the wind.
Even they can't survive way up here,
Where only a week, a day, maybe only an hour away,
The snow will come, and the earth here will be a cloud.

The mountains that ring this bowl are crafted of granite,
Of limestone, of rhyolite.
The word "mountains" does them no justice.
They are statues, monuments, chateaux in stone.
These words and yet no words describe these monoliths,
All gathered and bound together
By cements only God could muster.

Mounds of rock gather all around me,
Salt-and-pepper and rosy granite with bits of mica
Like diamond flakes a-glint in the sun.
Angular silver stones,
Poised on the brink of eternity beneath a sky
Of some blue they haven't invented a name for.

Royal blue, azure blue, turquoise, cornflower, sapphire:
Perhaps the sum of them all would equal this sky.

God made this summit piece by piece.
He carved each rock with care.
He excavated each lake
And mixed the blues and greens himself,
Finishing them off with a sprinkle of diamond dust.
He set each blade of grass in its realm,
Carved each troubled tree in the valley below
With the wind and rain as his only tools.

I am thankful to be a poet.
Thankful I can put a pen to paper
And release what builds inside me.
I fear if I couldn't that these emotions
Would build a dam across my soul forever.

Tears fill my eyes as I gaze over this spectacle.
Goose flesh takes over my skin.
Nothing could be so devoid of life as this place.
And yet nothing could be so full of life.
Spirits move here, the spirits of all the ages.

Those who come here come knowing they are someplace special.
Yet they have only an inkling.
There comes a time when all of them
Must walk somewhere to be alone.
Something about this place cannot be shared.
Man leaves his wife,
Woman her husband.
In stunned reverence they make their way to the brink,
The only sound the crunching of gravel beneath their feet.

I see a golden eagle, his wings unfurled,
Tilting expertly to move him this way and that.
He sees everything.
Perhaps he is the eyes of God.
I see a butterfly, lost, wandered out of its element into space,
Into peace, into Heaven.

What are the noises here?
A stone, nudged out of a place it has held since its creation,
Tips over the edge and rattles on rocks
As it descends until for several seconds there is silence.
Then a cold distant echo off the fractured cliff faces as it strikes
bottom.

Life and death.
A raven glides by,
And he tries to voice his primitive caw.
It comes out as a gargled clucking,
Like a tongue flicked across the teeth.
The raven, too, for once, is speechless.
There is the crunch of gravel beneath feet,
One's own sighs,
One's heartbeats.
A voice carrying across from the other side of the canyon.
And the wind.
There are no other noises.

This place is made for peace.
Somewhere, perhaps, is a man
Who can grasp the significance of Bear Tooth.
That man is perfect.
Only perfection can grasp perfection.
Nothing can touch this place.
Artist's brush. Poet's pen. Author's mind. Nothing.

Nothing lives here. Everything lives here.
God lives here.
One raven finds his voice,
And in the distance he raises a call of awe.

All I Want

One day I had everything—
Money, health, and fame,
Without a care or worry,
I was on top of the game.
But then I fell from Life's graces,
And there wasn't a thing I could do;
I lost all I had—the money and fame,
And all I had left was you.

I looked for my lifelong friends,
But found I had none left;
I wandered alone in depression,
Feeling completely bereft.
I saw people dying, leaving the world,
And I wished that I could go too,
For looking around, at the life I once knew,
All I had left was you.

I cried at night, wishing things could be different—
What had become of my life?
Where once I had pleasure, and all things good,
All I had left was strife.
There were people around me, loving their lives,
While I felt alone and blue;
They had everything a person could want,
And all I had left was you.

In every dark cloud is a silver lining,
And in time I opened my eyes;
I'd been mourning the loss of the fame and the wealth,
While holding onto a prize.
I didn't need all of the friends I once had,
For the luckiest number is two;
When I opened my eyes, I had all I wanted,
And all that I wanted was you.

I've Been Alive Forever

I've been alive forever,
Since the first forbidden fruit
Since the ark sailed on the waters,
Full of flying bird and brute.

I've been alive forever,
So I saw Goliath fall;
And I was there when they murdered Christ,
And darkness covered all.

Sadly, I saw the Crusades unfold,
And I knew it had to be,
But I wept to see the bodies strewn
And the blood that flowed so free.

I've been alive forever,
To watch ancestors sail
Across the broad blue ocean
To a land so young and hale.

High in a tree, I watched them come,
With flutes and drums in the dawn—
The proud Red Coats and the ones they fought,
Whose freedom would go on.

A troop of men, and a native girl

Trekked across the country wide,
To reach the edge of the continent,
To see the other side.

On grassy fields, in the war-torn East,
I saw the Gray and Blue,
Marching against each other—
Brothers, brave and true.

And on the high plains, in grass knee-high,
I saw a wave of horns
And the native people standing hopeless
As their home from them was torn.

I've watched a hundred wars,
And a million lives be lost,
Wept at the graves of the good and bad,
As I tried to count the cost.

I'm still here, but the world has changed,
And we're growing every day;
Too many souls clog the planet now,
And some have no place to stay.

Where skies were blue and grass grew tall,
There are brown skies now, and steel,
Concrete, asphalt, and plastic,
All with a lifeless feel.

I've been alive forever,
Seen glory and bitter pain;
I've seen agony and anger,
Joy and sun, and acid rain.

And if I had the chance
I don't know if I'd go again,
To see this pristine planet
Be wracked with war and strain.

I've been alive forever,
But my feet now turn to dust;
My body's gone to sickness,
And my weapons of war to rust.

I long to go back flying
To the place from where I came,
Before the world was a battlefield,
And the Earth was filled with shame.

The carnage I have witnessed
Will live forever now,
And I only pray that Mankind
Can survive it all somehow.

I've been alive forever;
I now go to my grave,
Worn, and tired and weary,
For the blood and tears I gave.

98

Introduction: More than ten years after its first writing, having gotten into cowboy poetry, which is almost always rhyming, I decided my poem "New Frontier" would probably sound better as a rhyming piece, so I set out to find out one way or the other. You've read the un-rhyming version. Here is version two:

New Frontier (In Rhyme)

They say this is the new age—
They call it civilization;
Which simply means there's not
A free spot left in this great nation;
Towering buildings jut up high,
Dirty, gray, and tall;
The sight of this new age sickens me
As I gaze upon it all.

Rockets, bombs, computers—
They call it all technology;
It's left me in a world of hurt—
For all I know's "cow-ology."
Those rockets flew so far away
One landed on the moon,
A place I thought God had reserved
For lovers to watch while they croon.

There are highways wider than a town,
They tell me they're called freeways;
Folks drive on them every day,

But for me there's only three ways:
One is if I'm dead and gone
And riding in a hearse;
Another's when I'm heading west,
Because the east is getting worse.

The last way you will find me there,
I must admit it now,
Is when I'm chasing after
Some stupid fence-jumping cow.
But I'd just as soon they broke them up
And put them back in dirt;
I cried when I saw I-Fifteen come through—
It made my spirit hurt.

There's a couple other words I've heard:
One's improvement and one's progress;
But I'm a cowboy, and when I look on this,
All I see is one big mess;
Improvement conquered the Rockies,
The Sierras, and Death Valley;
And by the time we sane folk knew,
The time had passed to rally.

Where did this all start, I wonder?
Was it with old Henry Ford?
He made a metal monster
Probably cursed even by the Lord;
They replaced those wagons and buggies
Folks used to hitch to horses
With sheets of unwieldy,
If shapely steel, drawn by inner forces.

There's no place on my sacred land,

Where if you glance back east
You won't look upon a freeway,
At a thousand smoking beasts;
They're even going off-road,
Trampling stream and brush,
Going places they don't know,
But going in a rush.

The trails of jeeps and motorbikes
Cut across hill and dale now,
Where years ago you'd only see
A mule deer, elk, or cow;
There was a time, upon this land,
There roamed the grizzly and bighorn sheep;
The eagle nested in the crags,
But forever they're asleep.

I guess first the roving Indian
And the mountain man saw their end,
When from the east the trails
Of a million settlers began to wend;
That's been over a hundred years,
And Jim Bridger now lies dead;
He never knew this civilization
Would be driving over his head.

Then in came the cowboy,
The survivor who couldn't die;
But settlers came and pretty soon
Death was glaring in his eye;
I guess that it's ironic:
The Indians looked over this nation,
And when the cowboy's hold was strong,
They called that civilization.

But pretty soon those cowboys
Found their time had come and went;
It made a lot of punchers weep,
When they saw their freedom spent;
The thirties came and then the forties,
Fifties, and the sixties;
And we got a bunch of crazy folks
Who think it's all just nifty.

To see a man land on the moon,
To brave the last frontier;
But for me it clenched my guts
And crammed my stomach full of fear;
For now I guess there's not
But one place that is safe—
And that's Heaven, where a lot of modern folk
Couldn't show their face.

Yes, they call this civilization,
And let them call it what they will;
But they killed the land and couldn't
Leave one damn rock standing still;
I'm sitting in a city—
Lord, tell me why I'm here;
Take me on to Heaven—
They can keep their new frontier.

Introduction: In 2016, with only the first two books in my Savage Law series under my belt, and my readers begging for more, my writing ceased, vanished along with my inspiration. In this horribly helpless mental environment of depression, where fiction cannot live, this sad poem was born . . .

A Helpless Author

My heart pounds;
I take a breath and it almost hurts;
My mind is numb to all thought—
All thought except the depressing reality of no thought . . .
My fingers move on a keyboard,
But only to reply to posts, comments, funny memes;
Creating with words is gone,
A forgotten art;
The longer I go without writing,
The deeper I sink into my inability to create;
The longer I go without writing,
The more I feel the death of my soul.
Sleepiness overcomes me;
But sleep is restless;
The knowledge that my edge is slipping
Plagues me worse than anything in the world.
I would walk through a snake den
Before I would choose this helpless blockage
Of my creative mind;
I would jump out of a perfectly good airplane
If I thought that act would rid me of writer's block

Forever . . .

Take this cup from me;
I want to write again;
I want to create;
I want to speak for the people I've created,
People whose mouths are essentially sewn shut
Unless I can overcome what has me tied:
Coal, Maura, Annie, Kathy, Connie, Jim…
They are waiting, reaching out to me,
Their faces full of anguish and fading hope,
Slowly sliding farther and farther away;
And I can't help them.
Heaven help a helpless author….

104

Introduction: Pondering on the loss of the woman I consider my second mother, Deanne Darger, made me think of all the other dear people I have lost in my life, and this poem came out of that lonely feeling of beloved people gone too soon.

They Might Be Gone

They might be gone,
Just an old memory;
Beneath some stone,
Part of history.

They might be gone,
And all that remains
Is a face on a wall
And the sound of their names.

They might be gone,
And all the cold tears
You cry for them
Can't turn back the years.

They might be gone,
And yet they live
In those they bore,
In the love you give.

They might be gone,

Yet they linger on,
Always beloved,
Waiting beyond.

They might be gone,
But in every dawn,
In every whisper,
They carry on.

Introduction: After a long battle with a malignant brain tumor, my cowboy friend Brian lost the fight, much to my shock and surprise. Brian's death led to a lot of verse as I tried to understand the loss of a man small of stature but so large of heart.

The Cowboy—Too Tough to Die

I can't believe he's gone—
The cowboy rode too tall to die;
Now he's sitting that old saddle,
Riding herd up in the sky.
He didn't stand too tall of stature;
Some might have even called him small;
But it's what's inside that really counted,
And he was taller than them all.

I can't believe it beat him,
That hungry beast that knows no friends;
But the cowboy kept on laughing,
Right up to the bitter end.
He never lost his humor—
Never lost his sense of love;
And we know he's standing guard now,
On his cow horse up above.

I can't believe he rode on,
To ranges way up in the sky;
To tell the truth, I thought he'd beat it,

And he'd keep on riding high.
Now tall in the saddle he smiles,
Up on the mountain called Scout;
Even if that funeral pyre
Claims our cowboy has bucked out.

He left a wife and family
Who will fly his banner high;
Who will long to see him smiling,
From his saddle in the sky.
And the friends who called him brother
Will keep the campfire burning bright;
For the buckaroo we all loved dearly,
Who rides the sky tonight.

We will miss our compañero,
Till the angels call us home;
For he left us way too young,
Those far-off ranges for to roam.
We will hear him in the thunder,
And in the breeze's sigh;
We will miss our smiling partner
Till we see him up on high.

The Cowboy's Blanket

There's a cowboy's blanket
At the foot of my bed,
In bold, bright colors,
Blue and red.

That cowboy's blanket,
It kept him warm;
Kept the winds at bay,
And the snowflakes' swarm.

That cowboy's blanket,
Red like blood,
Has laid on the bed ground
In the snow and mud.

It rode with him
On every horse he sat—
A cowboy's friend,
Like his spurs or hat.

A good stock saddle
Is a cowboy's prize,
But it can't warm him
Under nighttime skies.

That old red blanket

Was his gift to me,
For he couldn't take it
To eternity.

But now it's time,
And I think it best,
That the cowboy's blanket
Comes home to rest.

Cowboy Ride On

He was a cowboy;
He rode the range.
He loved his family;
That will never change.
He loved his country;
He loved his God;
In good times or bad times
The best trails he trod.

Cowboy, ride on—
You have fought your fires
On the range below;
Now you're climbing higher.
You spoke your mind;
On hard roads you trod;
You only had
To please your God.
Cowboy, ride on;
There are no fires in the sky;
Cowboy, ride on
To your reward on high.
Cowboy, ride on;
You have made your stand;
You came to earth
To ride for God's brand.

Our cowboy had to ride away,
And we still miss him to this very day;
But he's not gone;
He's out there still.
Watching over us
From some wind-swept hill.

Cowboy, ride on
To that golden land,
And the sagebrush hills
Made by God's hand.
We'll wait for you
At this campfire bright
While you explore
Those halls of light.
Cowboy, ride on
The great range in the sky;
Cowboy, ride on
Those trails on high.
Cowboy, ride on—
We'll see you soon.
Cowboy, ride on
Over the moon.
Cowboy, ride on
Over the moon.

I Used to Do That

A young man racing down a rocky hill;
I watch him on his horse, and my heart stands still;
The wind is blowing back his hat;
I used to sit a horse like that.

But then Father Time stepped in,
Gave me a punch right on the chin,
And now I'm like all old men,
With my bones all growing thin.
I lie here on the mat, remembering:
I used to do that.

A big red engine racing by;
Siren wailing and lights on high;
They'll quench some house fire in minutes flat;
I used to go in fires like that.

But then Father Time stepped in,
Gave me a punch right on the chin,
And now I'm like all old men,
With my bones all growing thin.
I lie here on the mat, remembering:
I used to do that.

Pounding up a mountain in a hot dry wind;
Racing against twenty other men

Toward a wildfire raging beyond control,
Like Satan calling for my soul!

But now Father Time stepped in,
Gave me a punch right on the chin,
And now I'm like all old men,
With my bones all growing thin.
I lie here on the mat, remembering:
I used to do that.

Song for a Pard

The stars are breaking loose
As if let out of their cages,
And I smell the scent of wilderness
Drift down from the ages;
There's an eerie yellow eastern glow
That'll light these hills up soon—
The glowing, laughing, spotted face
Of the globe they call the moon.

The campfire crackles bright
And hurls out a spark
That dances in the starlight
Till it dies out in the dark.
Leaves whisper around me
As the breeze whips them about,
And from the coals I catch the scent
Of two small sizzling trout.

Eyes flit in the forest—
My two horses and a mule—
The latter's what you always
Took out packing, as a rule;
I pick up your guitar and strum out
"Riding Down the Canyon,"
And I try to hold my tears back,

And all my cares abandon.

You would have loved this night,
But it's only me alone here;
A dog and three hoofed compañeros
Are all that's hanging near.
But your ghost is always with me,
Pard, and though I cannot see you,
I know you're walking through these woods
And looking out for me, too.

The sickness took you from me
When I was still a kid,
Leaving me the tales
Of all the things you did.
I sit next to the dying fire
And sing a trail song to your spirit,
Daddy, I pray God let you come
To sit by me and hear it

Gray

The day is gray, gray like my heart;
Thunder grumbles, and it speaks to me;
It tells me she is gone.
The rain, falling like my tears,
Patters on the roof;
It's a spring rain, and I should be happy.
The flowers will relish it,
And in time it will find itself
On display in their beauty.
But the colors won't mean so much;
I am seeing now in black and white—
And gray.

Thundersong

The earth smells clean, all washed by rain;
The thunder grumbles his disdain;
The lightning paints the forest floor
A silvery blue like nights before.
But no less silver is the moon,
An accent to the wind-sung tune.

Which one awoke me, I can't tell,
The thunder voice or the earthy smell,
The lightning's glare or the smiling moon,
The wind that's howling way too soon.
It's not my choice to wake just now,
But I lie awake and wonder how.

I try to stir my fire to life,
Using the blade of my Bowie knife,
But the rain that hisses in the coals
Puts the fire out, and the thunder rolls.
I wonder if my beaten hat
Will be enough with rain like that.

This cold gnaws bone, and gives me no slack,
As I sit and dream of your hair of black.
The storm growls at my nervous horse;
I hear him nicker, and the rain I curse.
The lightning flares in rain-drenched clouds,

And the thunder's voice is growing loud.

God's own kaleidoscope is in the sky,
And his own choir sings up on high.
The one's the lightning, the other the wind,
And the thunder is a drum corps, the lightning's kin.
Me, I'm just a lonely man, my heart is reaching out for you;
But it was you who left me alone and blue.

Do you feel the thunder rumble?
Do you hear the mountains grumble?
Do you wonder if I ever call your name?
Do you hear this wind that's sighing,
Does this rain beat on your roof?
Do you wake to hear me crying,
Or have you kept yourself aloof?

I cannot make you hear my pleading,
No more than I can cease the thunder's roll,
I can't reach you in this darkness
That's filling up my soul.
You have gone into a place, girl,
Where I cannot reach you now.
And I have to heal my bleeding heart,
And stop the pain somehow.

Now the moon hangs in a velvet sky,
And its company is the stars;
And once again it's flirting
With Jupiter and Mars;
The clouds that brought the lightning
Have all slipped beyond the veil
Of the world that lies surrounding me;
And the lonely coyote's wail

Is the song that brings me closer
To the God there up above
Who's the only one who can heal me
From these wounds of broken love.
I gave you all I had, my love, even all my soul;
I guess your answer was the lightning,
And the thunder's mighty roll.

The Lady Rides Horses

She don't care if she has to muck
She doesn't mind forking out hay.
She watches the horses gallop and buck;
She'll be flying on mountains today.

She walks through hell;
She don't know why;
She's just been trampled by another guy.
If she sticks with horses there'll come a day
She'll ride to heaven—her very own way.

And she rides—the lady rides horses;
And she glides—she glides on the wind;
And she flies—she flies with the eagles,
When the lady rides horses again.

I don't care if I have to muck;
And I don't mind forking out hay.
I watch the horses gallop and buck;
They'll be flying on mountains today.

I've watched that girl
Wading through hell;
I've felt that feeling—in fact I know it well;
So I keep praying, though at times it's tough,
She'll know I love her, and I'll be enough.

And she rides—the lady rides horses;
And she glides—she glides on the wind;
And she flies—she flies with the eagles,
When the lady rides horses again.

I want to ride when the lady rides horses;
I want to glide with her on the wind.
I want to fly as she flies with the eagles,
And just be with the lady
When she rides horses again.
My little lady, she rides horses again.

I'll Ride Until I Die

Until I die, I'll ride;
I'll ride until I die;
Then you can look for me
In the fading evening sky.

My daddy was a rider;
My mama loved him true;
She set me on a wild horse—
A horse we called Old Blue.

To the far skyline I rode,
And I won my mama's awe;
She said I could ride a cyclone—
The same way as my pa.

Until I die, I'll ride;
I'll ride until I die;
Then you can look for me
In the wink of a mustang's eye.

I broke my first wild horse
At just seven years old;
Bought with money I found free:
A silver sky and sunset gold.

I've never owned a house;

I've never owned a car;
But I own the mountains high,
And I own the prairies far.

Until I die, I'll ride;
I'll ride until I die;
Then you can look for me
On a ghost mustang on high.

I'll go out with a bang;
I'll buck out with a yell;
I'll be riding on some mustang
Like a cyclone out of hell.

There'll be nothing left of me,
Nothing but a song
Sung by other cowboys
With ev'ning shadows growing long.

Until I die, I'll ride;
I'll ride until I die;
Keep listening for me
In a cold blue norther's sigh.

Ty-yo-ho! Ty-Yay-hay!
I'll ride the prairie o'er;
Until my dying day.

Until I die, I'll ride,
Sitting straight up as a rod;
And then you all can find me
Training wild mustangs for God.

Until I die, I'll ride;

I'll ride until I die;
Then you can look for me
In the fading evening sky.

I'll be riding way on high!

Our Autumn

The sun pours down the mountain;
The river winds below;
The sun makes dappled shadows
From the aspens all a-glow.

A stubborn, struggling maple
Refuses to go down;
She holds tight to the glory
Of her scarlet-colored crown.

A bugle from the timber
Floats across the canyon deep,
From some ruler of his harem,
In his misty mountain keep.

Way high up in the heaven,
Geese honking, on the wing,
Like distant, misshaped beads,
Gone wild off their string.

The morning smells like honey,
The firs like potpourri;
Even the forest loam
Adds to fragrant ecstasy.

Autumn is upon us now,

In bursts of red and gold,
Forest life is burgeoning
With stories yet untold.

But soon arrives the winter,
With its cold and ice and snow;
Bringing silence to these mountains
And the valleys down below.

So stop and take a deep breath,
And enjoy these autumn gifts;
Revel in the life and beauty
As the peace around you sifts.

Your life is like the autumn,
With its glory and its sun;
So fleetingly it passes,
And your autumn will be done.

There is no time for sadness;
There is no time for woe;
Relish in those you love dearly,
Before your time to go.

A Cottage So White

The path broke off from the town road there,
And we two followed with nary a care;
It drew us on, as if by a charm;
We strolled along, arm in arm.

And then we spied it—the cottage so white;
The windows shimmered in soft sunlight;
The house was surrounded by a dainty low fence—
The cottage that charmed us and warmed every sense.

All shuttered and barred, no one home, we could tell;
We went up the walk, as if caught in a spell;
The grass so green and flowers gold
The love of someone completely told.

We felt the urge to hurry on,
Moving across the unmown lawn;
And behind the house, so tidy and clean,
We spied a meadow, lush and green.

To our eyes, a most beautiful sight,
With all its flowers, lovely and bright;
They were gold and scarlet, violet and blue,
Bluebirds on high, and robins, too.

We walked along in knee-high grass,

Praying this moment would never pass;
And then we stopped, and made sweet love there,
While a soft, gentle breeze played in our hair.

That small, fleeting moment, that bond of our lives,
It overcame us, both me and my wife;
And the beauty around us, the blue sky above
Strengthened our undying love.

But when it was over, with the sun slipping down,
We followed the silent lane back to town;
We will remember, in fond thoughts and dreams,
The bird songs above us, and a meadow of green;
And as we grow old, if our minds should grow slight,
There will still live within us a cottage so white.

Somewhere There's a Meadow

Somewhere there's a meadow,
In autumn's waving gold,
In winter's snowy blanket, ·
Or springtime's verdant fold;
In summer it is full of life,
Flowers, grass, and trees;
Aspen, pine, and maple,
Kissed by fragrant breeze.

No one sees the meadow,
For no one knows it's there;
Only I and I alone,
Here in Nature's lair.
But I would take you with me, dear,
If you would take my hand,
To show you through my paradise,
This undiscovered land.

Wheels cannot find this place,
But human feet alone;
I'll help you cross a babbling stream,
Across its polished stones.
Pretty flowers will greet your eyes,
Waving grass your feet,
And I will take you in my arms
And kiss your lips so sweet.

Towering pines will guard us—
Aspen look away;
Lupine and Indian paintbrush
Will bloom for us that day;
I share with you my meadow, dear,
In hopes that we'll be one;
We've shared so many hopes and dreams,
In the many things we've done.

I'm not a man of promises,
I hope you understand—
But I want to press your heart to mine,
Forever hold your hand;
Now you know my meadow, girl,
You and only you;
I've shared with you a secret
Meant for only two;
So close your eyes and take my hand;
At least give us a try;
Please don't forget my meadow,
Or here my dream will die.

The Spring

Long ago, when I was young,
I wandered far—searching, discovering,
Finding the small mysteries that life
Held in store for me.
I was pleased by the simple things then;
Nothing complicated—the little gifts of God.
A frog in a rain puddle;
A soft, wiggly pup;
A big, colorful fish at the end of a line;
A soft, warm rain whispering across a window pain,
Pattering on a tin roof.

As I grew, though, life became more complicated,
As life does.
I needed bigger things to please me.
Bigger toys;
Faraway places;
Things of the world.
It was then I found the spring:
Gurgling, bubbling, mountain cold and crystal clear,
It raced from the darkness of a stone,
Feeding its beauty to the world.
Though the spring didn't fit into my busy world,
It pleased me by its newness,
Its gentle, easy course.
It made me happy when nothing else could.

It gave me warmth,
Treated me as its friend,
As if it would never let me down.

Sadly, the things of the world had drawn my mind,
And ignoring my love for the spring,
I went away, with no more than a gentle word,
A faint suggestion of return.
It took me forever, it seems,
To see what the spring offered—
That it, in fact, meant life to me.
I finally learned that the things of this life were nothing,
That the spring was everything.
But it was a dry, lonely time for the spring,
As I was out discovering the world.
They tell me the spring is drying up,
It may be gone from me.
As I make my way back with all my speed,
I hope and pray that the spring is yet there,
That it has yet a little to offer me—
A little love, a little hope.
For if I return to what once was home
Only to find that the spring is no more,
I beg the grave to take me,
For my joy is gone.
If the spring is dry,
My life, too, will go dry.

I'll Never Die

There may come an end
Of you seeing me;
I may wander on
Up into the sky.
I may change my form
To a bird or a tree,
But I promise you
That I'll never die.

No, I'll never die;
I'll live in the wind;
I'll walk in the forest,
And the sunshine I'll send.
As a mustang I'll run;
As an eagle I'll fly;
I'll watch from the moon;
No, I'll never die.

I wish you could see
Me here by your side;
I'd like you to know
I won't say goodbye.
I wish you'd not tell
Your friends that I died,
I'm with you for good,
And I'll never die.

No, I'll never die;
I'll live in the wind;
I'll walk in the forest,
And the sunshine I'll send.
As a mustang I'll run;
As an eagle I'll fly;
I'll watch from the moon;
No, I'll never die.

And I'll shine on the mountain, in fresh snow;
I'll run and I'll play up in the clouds;
I pray that you always will know:
As thunder, I will call your name out loud.

No, I'll never die;
I'll live in the wind;
I'll walk in the forest,
And the sunshine I'll send.
As a mustang I'll run;
As an eagle I'll fly;
I'll watch from the moon;
No, I'll never die.

I'll watch you from the moon;
No, I'll never die.

Footprints in the Sand

Tiny footprints in the sand,
Tiny touch of a child's hand,
Tiny castles crumbling down,
This tiny world keeps spinning 'round.

Calling seagulls in the sky,
Glowing sunsets in my eye;
Sunny days, and moonlit nights,
Soon my babies are out of sight.

They are tiny, they are small,
But they grow up, and then they're tall;
They are little—and they want their mom;
But I turn around, and now they're gone.

Little cheeks had too much sun;
Little feet, always on the run;
Little eyes are watching me,
Yet their future I cannot see.

Floating boats out on the sea;
A little voice shares them with me;
A little hand, so meek in mine,
But they grow up, with Father Time.

They were tiny, they were small,

But they grew up, and now they're tall;
I watched them grow beside their mom;
But they grew up, and now they're gone.

A tiny pup held in their arms
Thinks that he is safe from harm;
He's in peril deep, but he doesn't see;
I guess that pup is blind as me.

Tiny thoughts, big as the moon,
Tiny dreams will come true soon;
Tiny beds get way too small,
When tiny babies grow way too tall.

They were tiny, they were small;
I looked away, and now they're tall.
I miss those years we'd watch them grow;
I wish they never had to go.

Tiny tears, here on my face,
Staring at this empty place;
I guess it's all part of the plan;
They grow and leave fast as they can.

And we cry—we're babies too,
With no idea just what to do;
Tiny hands held in our hands
Are gone, like footprints in the sand.

TRIBUTES

TO

MOTHER

There When I Cry

A letter I hold in my hand tonight,
A mem'ry I hold in my heart;
The letter says, "I love you,
And it's sad to be apart."

I fly to a time when I was young,
When all the world was mine,
When my mother held me in her arms
And told me all was fine.

I remember a creek that ran by our lane,
I remember gold leaves in the fall;
I remember a hand holding mine so tight,
My mother above me so tall.

I was in Heaven, back in those days—
The world was a playground bright;
Mother would take me walking by day,
And she'd read me to sleep in the night.

We went to the yard in the winter
To build up a big man of snow;
We'd retreat when the sun started fading,
And listen to howling winds blow.

We shared many hours together,

Music, reading, and games;
We'd visit all of the people she knew,
Though now I've forgotten their names.

Carefree days of my youth are now gone;
I couldn't hold on, or I'd try;
But even all these years gone by,
My mother's still there when I cry.

A Long and Winding Road

It's a long and winding road we tread,
That leads to Heaven's door—
Over some rocks and pits and ruts,
And for some a whole lot more.
There are tires flat and motors burned,
Heels and toes worn raw;
We look ahead, across the endless miles,
And we sit and stare with awe.

There are things that make that road more rough,
But some make it more smooth,
Like a touch from one we love so dear,
Or the healing words that soothe.
I have to say, in all my years,
There's a beam that lit my way;
There's a gentle smile, a guiding hand
That made everything okay.

Recall that road which seemed so long
Precious years gone by?
Remember a kiss upon your cheek?
Or a baby's restful sigh?
I guess the road's not all that long,
For we look back with a smile;
The rocks and ruts and potholes—
Precious mem'ries every mile.

Mother

The sky is blue this evening,
Like the mem'ries sleeping now
Of a mother sweet and gentle,
With sweat upon her brow—

The sweat of hours of labor,
Of toil she did for love,
For five children who lay dreaming,
And for Father up above.

The past, they say, is in the past,
No way to change its course;
But I look back with an aching heart,
Brimming with remorse.

Tears fall on these words I write,
As I try to understand
The love there in those creases
In battered, calloused hands.

I guess you never comprehend,
Until it grows too late,
Until the path's been chosen
By the rock-hard hand of fate;

I wonder why we never tried

To lend a helping hand,
Or tried to ease that aching soul
As she fought to make a stand.

Regret is such a frail word,
But the only one I know
To demonstrate my feelings,
And in some way to show

That if I had them over,
Those years with my dear friend,
I'd try to help along the way
To reach a happy end.

Mom, I hope you somehow know
How much I care for you,
That I would give my life for you,
Dear Mom, please know it's true.

For Mom

Age. They say it brings wisdom.
Wisdom? I don't know.
But I do know it brings memories.
Memories and regrets.

I wish I had a dollar
For each time Mother helped me;
I'd give them all back now,
Hoping in some way to help her, too.

No one ever cared like Mom;
But I was shy and quiet,
And many things I never said.
Now I regret.

Age must bring wisdom.
At least for some.
It brought Mother wisdom.
If only I had used hers those many times I cried alone.

I'm older now. I'm not supposed to cry.
Why do I then?
Why do I sit alone, think of times past,
And cry till I cannot see?

I guess because I'm sorry;

Sorry for the times I let slip through my fingers—
Sorry for the unkind words I said,
Or the unkind thoughts I thought.

Somewhere in this universe
There's a place where all the regrets are stored;
My storage space is large, the rent dear;
I want to trade mine in.

I want to trade my regrets today,
Trade them for chances.
Chances to love my mother more,
To love my wife and children more.

Chances to feel the wind in my hair,
Standing on one of God's lovely mountains
With autumn leaves on the trees below
And a sparkling river in the distance.

I don't know if age will bring me wisdom,
The way it did my mom;
But let it give me instinct, at least,
To know the best way, the best time,
To show my love.
And then to do it every chance I get.

146

Introduction: In September 2020, with my mother having reached the age of eighty-two, I steadied her as she walked slowly toward the passenger side of a car my brother would drive, and I thought of the vibrant young woman who took, almost at a run, the tower stairs at the factory where she worked. This mortal life makes me ache when I see a once strong and confident woman fumble her way through her existence, waiting just to go . . .

Steps

I took my first steps, and she was there;
Steps on hard, dark wood, on carpet firm;
I made my first tracks in snow, and hers were there;
On the Atlantic shore I left indentations of my toes in the sand;
She left hers beside them.
On dusty eastern paths,
In giant, magical stores full of childhood dreams I walked;
Always her footsteps trod beside mine.

I kicked my first gold and red leaves of autumn
Before I was old enough to understand where the green had gone,
And she was standing there holding my hand, trying to explain;
In the vastness of museums too monumental to comprehend,
She held my hand, carrying me when I grew tired;
When the crack in front of the escalator
Threatened to swallow me whole,
She patiently smiled, took my hand, and saved my life.

She was beside me through my childhood terrors,
Facing hordes of strange children in grade school,
Hordes like I had never seen.
She stood beside me through fevers,
And after mind-numbing nightmares;
She refereed my first fight,
Letting me keep my pride by not stepping in.
And when it was time to complete a long ago-started journey
And walk the sands of the Pacific, she was walking with me too.

I grew and walked many steps without her then—
Up the aisle to receive a diploma,
Down the narrow cobblestones, grand avenues,
And hallowed, war-torn beaches of far-off France,
On myriad calls with a gun on my hip or a firehose in my hands.
I traveled thousands and thousands of miles alone,
Because she had made me strong.

Now my steps are strong and sure,
And hers are slow and hesitant;
Bright skies of my youth are dimming,
As I watch the one who brought me here struggle forward,
Steps tentative, jaw set firm.
My first steps I took in her presence;
Now I try to prepare to watch her take her last.
But no preparation is enough
For this step we all must take.

She will lay down her mortal coil forever
And take steps into a bright new realm,
While I will walk on, covering my tears with steps of my own.

Author's note

A huge thanks is owed to my son Clay, who helped me design the cover, "showing his quality"—a line all *Lord of the Rings* fans will recognize. Clay also typeset this book and helped me decide which poems to include and which to save for the next book. Thank you, Clay. You have become such a tremendous part of my heart and soul.

About the Author

Kirby Frank Jonas was born in 1965 in Bozeman, Montana. His earliest memories are of living seven miles outside of town in a wide crack in the mountains known as Bear Canyon. At that time it was a remote and lonely place, but a place where a boy with an imagination could grow and nurture his mind, body and soul.

From Montana, the Jonas family moved almost as far across the country as they could go, to Broad Run, Virginia, to a place that, although not as deep in the timbered mountains as Bear Canyon was every bit as remote—Roland Farm. Once again, young Jonas spent his time mostly alone, or with his older brother, if he was not in school. Jonas learned to hike with his mother, fish with his father, and to dodge an unruly horse.

Jonas moved to Shelley, Idaho, in 1971, and from that time forth, with the exception of a few sojourns elsewhere, he became an Idahoan. Jonas attended all twelve years of school in Shelley, graduating in 1983. In the sixth grade, he penned his first novel, *The Tumbleweed,* and in high school he wrote his second, *The Vigilante.* It was also during this time that he first became acquainted with Salmon, Idaho, staying toward the end of the road at the Golden Boulder Orchard and taking his first steps to manhood.

Jonas has lived in six cities in France, in Mesa, Arizona, and explored the United States extensively. He has fought fires for the Bureau of Land Management in five western states and carried a gun on his hip in three different jobs.

In 1987, Jonas met his wife-to-be, Debbie Chatterton, and in 1989 took her to the altar. Over some rough and rocky roads they have traveled, and across some raging rivers that have at times threatened to draw them under, but they survived, and with four beautiful children to show for it: Cheyenne, Jacob, Clay and Matthew.

Jonas has been employed as a Wells Fargo armored guard, a wildland firefighter, a security guard for California Plant Protection and Inter-Con, and police officer. He is now retired after almost twenty-four years of proud employment as a municipal firefighter for the city of Pocatello, Idaho, and works full-time job as a private security officer guarding the federal courthouse under contract with the security company Paragon.

One of Jonas's greatest joys in life is watching his second son, Clay, become a recognized writer of much talent in his own chosen field, that of fantasy and science fiction, with his current series *The Descendants of Light*. There is no greater compliment a son could give to his father than to follow in his footsteps.

Books by Kirby Jonas

Season of the Vigilante, Book One: The Bloody Season
Season of the Vigilante, Book Two: Season's End
The Dansing Star
Legend of the Tumbleweed
Lady Winchester
The Devil's Blood
The Secret of Two Hawks
Knight of the Ribbons
Drygulch to Destiny
Samuel's Angel
The Night of My Hanging (And Other Short Stories)
Russet
A Final Song for Grace

Savage Law series
1. *Law of the Lemhi, part 1*
   Law of the Lemhi, part 2
2. *River of Death*
3. *Lockdown for Lockwood*
4. *Like a Man Without a Country*
5. *Thunderbird*
6. *Savage Alliance*

The Badlands series
1. *Yaqui Gold* (co-author Clint Walker)
2. *Canyon of the Haunted Shadows*

Legends West series
1. *Disciples of the Wind* (co-author Jamie Jonas)
2. *Reapers of the Wind* (co-author Jamie Jonas)

Lehi's Dream series
1. *Nephi Was My Friend*
2. *The Faith of a Man*
3. *A Land Called Bountiful*
4. *Shores of Promise* (forthcoming)

Gray Eagle series (e-book format only—forthcoming in print)
1. *The Fledgling*
2. *Flight of the Fledgling*
3. *Wings on the Wind*
Death of an Eagle (e-book and large format softbound)

Books on audio

The Dansing Star, narrated by James Drury, *"The Virginian"*
Death of an Eagle, narrated by James Drury
Legend of the Tumbleweed, narrated by James Drury
Lady Winchester, narrated by James Drury
Yaqui Gold, narrated by Gene Engene
The Secret of Two Hawks, narrated by Kevin Foley
Knight of the Ribbons, narrated by Rusty Nelson
Drygulch to Destiny, narrated by Kirby Jonas

Available through the author at www.kirbyjonas.com

Email the author at: kirby@kirbyjonas.com or write to:

Howling Wolf Publishing
1611 City Creek Road
Pocatello ID 83204